When you go out on a
sunny day, your **shadow**
goes with you.

When you skip or
swing or run, your
shadow does, too.

If the sun shines in
front of you, your shadow
will be behind you.

If the sun shines behind
you, your shadow will be in
front of you.

Dogs and cats have
shadows. Cars and rocks
have shadows, too.

A few **clouds** in the sky
make shadows on the ground.

But if the sky is dark and
gray, it may be too cloudy
to find many shadows.

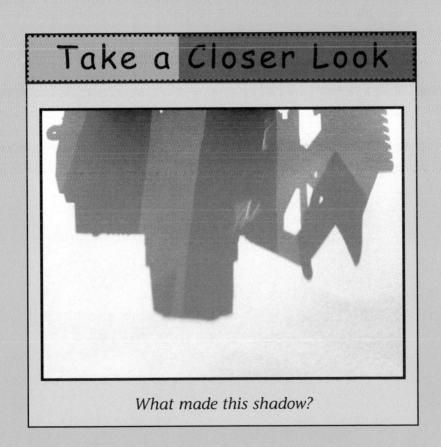

What made this shadow?

There must be **light** to make shadows. The sun makes very bright light.

A toy truck!

10

The sun's light comes from
its heat. Other hot things can
make light, too.

A fire makes light. Candles make light when they burn. Stars make light.

Electricity (i-lek-**triss**-uh-tee) makes light in lightbulbs. Even a tiny flashlight bulb can make bright light.

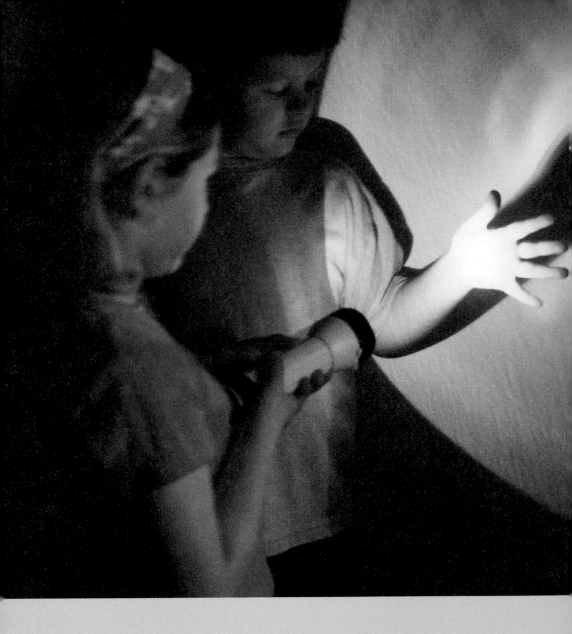

Take a flashlight into a
dark room. It can help you
learn more about shadows.

Shine the flashlight toward
a wall. Hold your hand in
front of the light.

The light shines on
your hand. But it cannot
shine *through* your hand.

Take a Closer Look

What made this shadow?

You make shadows on the wall when your hand blocks the light.

Hold a book, or a ball, or
a toy in front of the light.

A bicycle wheel!

Every shadow you see is made
by something that blocks light.

Shadows can be many **shapes.** And shadows can change shape. They can change from short to long, or long to short.

Noon

Three o'clock

Shadows can also change
from fat to thin, or thin to fat.
Sometimes shadows change
because of the time of day. At
noon, shadows are short. In the
morning, or in the afternoon,
shadows are longer.

Sometimes shadows change because the light or the object moves. Shine your flashlight on your hand. Keep the flashlight in the same spot, and see what happens when you move your hand.

Hold your hand close to the wall. Your shadow will look very small.

Move your hand closer to
the light. Your shadow will
get bigger.

Your shadow grows from
small to big because you are
blocking more light.

Bird

You can make pictures
with shadows.

Here are two you may want to try.

Dog

At night, there might be
enough light for shadows, too.

Light from the windows
of a store will make shadows.

Light from a streetlight, or
the moon, can make shadows
on your walls.

Before you go to sleep
tonight, try to find all the
shadows in your room.

If you fall asleep before
you are done, that is okay.
There will be more shadows
to find tomorrow!

Glossary

clouds—tiny bits of water, snow, dust, or ice that collect in the air

electricity (i-lek-**triss**-uh-tee)—a force that can make light

light—something bright that helps you see

shadow—a dark shape made by something that blocks light

shapes—the forms of things

A Note to Parents

Learning to read is such an exciting time in a child's life. You may delight in sharing your favorite fairy tales and picture books with your child.

But don't forget the importance of introducing your child to the world of nonfiction. The ability to read and comprehend factual material will be essential to your child in school and throughout life. The Scholastic Science Readers™ series was created especially with beginning readers in mind. These books, with their clear texts and beautiful photographs, will help you to share the wonders of science with *your* new reader.

Suggested Activity

Go on a "shadow search" with your child! You might start with a list of shapes to find, as if you were on a scavenger hunt. See if he or she can find a round shadow, a pointy shadow, a shadow that looks like a box, or other simple shapes. Search inside or out, but remember that you'll find some of the best shadows when you and your child are outside on a sunny day!